E.N.O.U.G.H.
Evil Never Overcomes Under God's Hand

By Mrs. Alruth Toney

Jewell Jordan Publishing LLC
Oklahoma

Copyright © 2025 Alruth Toney

All rights reserved. No part of this book may be used or reproduced in any manner without the Author's or the Publisher's written permission.

For information, address:
Jewell Jordan Publishing, LLC
1205 South Air Depot Blvd, Suite 153,
Midwest City, Oklahoma 73110

Interior design and cover design by Medina Isiah Designs, www.medinaisiah.com

Photograph courtesy of the Author
Image credit: GraysonStock - Adobe Stock

Library of Congress Control Number: 2025930519

Paperback ISBN: 978-1-7360906-7-1

First Edition

Printed in the United States of America

Dedication

To Seniors Everywhere

Contents

Foreword vii

A Word From the Author xi

Chapter 1: Raised By My Grandmother 15

Chapter 2: Work, Segregation and Education 19

Chapter 3: Beware: Lessons Learned 25

Chapter 4: Takeaways For Seniors and All Victims 49

Chapter 5: Enjoying Life In My 90s 57

Foreword

E.N.O.U.G.H.- EVIL NEVER OVERCOMES UNDER GOD'S HAND, by Mrs. Alruth Toney, is a story about one woman defining and demonstrating successful aging for herself through her acquired wisdom and unrelenting faith.

Successful aging is viewed as a dynamic process that considers the outcome of our development over the life course[1], and our ability to grow and learn by using past experiences to manage present circumstances, all while maintaining a realistic sense of who we are and what we can accomplish. A big part of successful aging is using the **wisdom** and bits of knowledge that we have developed over our lifetime.

Recently, while waiting for service at my auto repair shop, I overheard a conversation between a customer and the Service Advisor. The customer, a woman around my age (70-ish), asked the consultant several questions regarding her car repairs. Her questions were pointed and forcefully delivered, and she insisted on understanding the repair details. When she seemed satisfied with the ser-

---

[1] What is successful ageing and who should define it? BMJ 2005; 331 doi: https://doi.org/10.1136/bmj.331.7531.1548 (Published 22 December 2005) Cite this as: BMJ 2005; 331:1548.

vice proposed, she politely apologized for her tone and questioning attitude. She explained that she was newly widowed and had never had to take care of her car before, but she was committed to not being taken advantage of by anyone just because she was a widow, a woman, or an older adult.

I remember thinking in the moment… 'Do not apologize! You are asking the questions that any woman/man of any age or status should ask to ensure they get what they pay.' Unfortunately, elderly adults are often the target of swindles and fraudulent activities. The extent of this problem is demonstrated by the millions of senior citizens falling victim to financial exploitation and elder scams every year. According to the FBI's **elder scam statistics**[2], an estimated five million seniors are scammed yearly, with the total annual cost exceeding $36 billion. With these shocking numbers, focus is needed on developing awareness and implementing strategies to prevent the financial exploitation of elderly adults.

What is more, seniors who fall victim to financial scams often suffer from emotional distress, loss of independence, and compromised physical health, in addition to economic losses and family discord.

---

2 https://www.fbi.gov/news/stories/elder-fraud-in-focus#

Foreword

To Mrs. Toney's surprise, she realized that scams, cons, and misrepresentations do not only arise from "shady" individuals. Banks, credit unions, and other financial institutions—corporate conglomerates—play a huge role—whether it's redlining, important or contradictory terms hidden in the fine print, or advertisements and commercials that only provide you with some of the information, none or only a small portion of which is relevant. Sometimes it's not what they say, and sometimes it is what they don't.

In her decades-long battle to address lending and banking practices, she concluded that they were unfair, illegal, and blatantly biased against seniors. That is why Mrs. Alruth Toney insisted, at 94 years of age, that she would tell the world the details of the real estate saga that she had been living for 20 years.

In telling her story, you feel her emotions, her struggle with communication challenges, and her desire to gain satisfaction with business transactions as an older person.

Mrs. Toney states: *"The point is that the purchases I embarked upon in 2004 were no different and no more unusual than purchases made by hundreds of thousands of others. However, in my case, very little turned out as I expected or anticipated. Was I to blame? I don't think so. Was it because of my age? Perhaps, however, my journey is a warning for people of all ages. Scams are rampant these days, affecting all of us, but perhaps most particularly the so-called "elderly."*

E.N.O.U.G.H.

In her exceptionally detailed account of the events that led to her near-catastrophic financial ruin, Mrs. Toney's story includes examples of differences in values and perspectives of older adults that may influence how some older adults misinterpret the signals in business situations, leaving them more open to fraud. This tome also identifies strategies that older individuals can use to help them avoid her plight.

A myriad of studies on aging successfully point to one's wisdom as a strategy for overcoming the challenges that may confront older adults. Mrs. Toney's story reflects the wisdom she employed to ultimately resolve her financial challenges and repair her relationships with her family.

Dr. Wynell M. Neece, PhD

A Word From the Author

My name is Alruth Toney. I am 94 years old, turning 95 in June.

The reason for this book—my journey through scams, cons, and misrepresentations by banks and finance companies without sanction or relief from any local, state, or governmental agencies—began in 2004.

This all began twenty years ago when I was 74 years old. I had paid all my bills and the mortgage on my house, which my ex-husband and I purchased in 1957. Like other homeowners, through the years, I borrowed against the equity in my home for remodeling and repair projects—finishing the laundry room, a room add on, enclosing my home with a 6ft wooden fence, building a two-car garage, repaving my driveway, and twice changing out clay pipes in both the front and back yards with plastic pipes. I did not borrow the money for these repairs all at once or in one lump sum. Instead, I would borrow money from my then-banking institution—Public Service Credit Union (PSCU)—for a particular project and repay the loan before proceeding to a new project.

One day in 2004, I was listening to a KOA radio talk show hosted by Mike Rosen. Rosen was a well-known conservative talk show host and political commentator. I listened to his program to keep apprised of the conservative viewpoint and because Rosen often invited Denver's first African American mayor, Wellington Webb, onto his show to joust with him.

During a commercial break in his show on this day, Rosen advertised a fixed-rate, low-interest loan offered by American Financing Corporation (AFC). In touting the loan, Rosen assured listeners that he would recommend it to his daughter. The loan interested me because I had been considering buying a new car. I had already saved significant money for a downpayment ($17,000.00) and believed the loan would supplement my savings and expedite the process. I called the radio station and provided my contact information, which KOA submitted to AFC. That began a nightmare of scams, misrepresentation, and cons, which continued into 2024. To be sure, it has ended now, not because of admissions of wrongdoing or because I have recouped my losses, but because at 94, I am exhausted and unwilling to continue to disrupt the remainder of my life, beating my head against intransigent, and impenetrable corporate walls.

In the next chapters, I will recount the specifics of this nightmare. Once you read my story, it will be up to you to decide whether you believe me or discount me—as many senior citizens are discounted—because of my age.

But first, I want you to know a little about me . . .

CHAPTER 1

Raised By My Grandmother

My name is Alruth Bennett Toney. Bennett is the family name.

I was born in Aberdeen, Mississippi, but grew up in East St. Louis, Illinois. I am named after two aunts, Alberta and Annie Ruth. Putting those two names together made my name "Alruth."

I lived in East Saint Louis until I was 17, attending John Robinson and Dunbar Elementary schools, and Lincoln Junior and Senior High schools.

Reflecting on the last nearly 100 years, I now realize that those first 17 years were the best years of my life. I was much loved by my dear, dear grandmother, Margaret Ward. Admittedly, at the time, I felt different because my grandmother raised me, while most of my peers had their moms and dads. I was jealous of kids who had their moms and dads, and I just had a grandmother. But I regret feeling that way now that I know the difference between love by choice and love by responsibility.

My grandmother, whom I called Mama, had three sisters and two brothers. One of the sisters, Mabel Hampton, whose nickname was Aunt Sugar, had no children and sort of adopted me. She is responsible for my close walk with God because she made sure that I attended church and Sunday school. We would stay for morning service, then return for Baptist Training Union (BTU) in the late afternoon, and finally, evening service. Unless my cousins and I were excused to go to the movies, this was our routine. That was a special treat—it did not happen often, but we surely enjoyed those movies when we were excused to go to them on those certain Sundays.

I was baptized at Mount Zion Baptist Church at about 7 or 8 years old. I remember standing on the platform of the church—Mt. Zion was a brick building, two stories high, with the entrance on the 2nd floor. One had to climb about 6 feet or more of stairs to gain entrance to the sanctuary. On the day of my baptism, Easter Sunday morning, I remember coming out on the platform in a white organza dress, a new person, a little girl whose grandmother had raised her, and her grandmother and Lord were the only people who knew she existed.

Raised By My Grandmother

Aunt Sugar had a piano. I took piano lessons and would go to her house to practice on her piano. My ability to play the piano was another reason I was raised in the Church. I now deeply regret not continuing my piano lessons. I subsequently discovered I had a good singing voice, and had I been able to read music, I could have done a far better job singing by following the notes and staying on pitch.

Mama had five girls and one boy: I'm the product of the one boy. I'm also the first grandchild, which I think caused me to be spoiled a little bit.

After school and in the summer, I babysat Mama and Aunt Sugar's mother, my great-grandmother. During these early years, an endearment arose between the three of us— my great-aunt Sugar, my grandmother, and me, which is why I now say these were the best years of my life.

Today, I am 94 years young, and I want you to know me personally so you can be the judge. You can decide whether you believe me or discount me because of my age. Unfortunately, the latter is often the case for many senior citizens.

One final note on the impact of my walk with God. There is a song entitled *If It Had Not Been for the Lord on My Side*[1] by Helen Baylor , which I embraced during this most

---

1 If It Had Not Been For the Lord On My Side - Helen Baylor: Song Lyrics, Music Videos & Concerts (shazam.com)

difficult and challenging time in my life. And I know it is true. If It had not been for the Lord on my side, I have no idea where I would be. Without my faith, I can see I may have been in somebody's insane asylum at 74 years old just because I wanted to buy a car at what I believed to be a fixed, low-interest rate. Instead, because I was raised in the Church, I learned several bible verses that have helped me through the hills and valleys of life. One in particular helped me through the period I share with you in this book. The verse is Philippians 4:4-7:

> *4 Rejoice in the Lord always. I will say it again: Rejoice! 5 Let your gentleness be evident to all. The Lord is near. 6 Do not be anxious about anything, but in every situation, by prayer and petition, with thanksgiving, present your requests to God. 7 And the peace of God, which transcends all understanding, will guard your hearts and your minds in Christ Jesus.*

CHAPTER 2

Work, Segregation and Education

Education & Segregation

Despite being spoiled, I worked while attending high school and, in the summers, even before college. In addition to caring for my great-grandmother, Amanda Thompson, whom we called "Gramma" on weekends and summers, I also cleaned homes during high school. That work motivated me to complete my education and have a career.

I graduated from Lincoln High School in 1947 and was voted most likely to succeed, which I challenged at the time. Over the years, that title has sometimes plagued me and oftentimes pushed me.

I received a full scholarship to Illinois State Normal University (now Illinois State University), the oldest public university in Illinois. I am eternally grateful to Mr. Hughes

E.N.O.U.G.H.

Quinn, principal of Lincoln High School, for assisting me in receiving the scholarship.

Attending Illinois State Normal University (ISNU) in September 1947 was my first time away from home. This opportunity to go away to college was good for me, but it was very scary.

There were two cities in Illinois—Normal and Bloomington—separated by Main Street. Normal, Illinois, was where the ISNU campus was located and where mostly White people lived. In contrast, Bloomington, Illinois—about a forty-five-minute bus ride to campus—had a predominantly Black population. When I attended ISNU, Black people were prohibited from living in the dorms or on campus. So, Black students like me had to commute from Bloomington to Normal, IL. On very cold days, despite the weather and the laws of segregation that mandated I sit in the back of the bus for the rather long bus ride, I persevered.

The limitations imposed by segregation made my social life on campus almost non-existent. During my first year at ISNU, there was only one other Black student from East Saint Louis, Helen Appleby; she was an upperclassman. During my sophomore year, other Black students arrived to attend ISNU, making our social life a little more bearable. My experiences during those first two years led me to suggest to the ISNU administration that counseling be made available to new students—especially those students from all Black schools, for whom this was their first time in an integrated school. Unfortunately, this did not happen.

Despite the obstacles I faced in attending ISNU, I was determined to get out of East St. Louis, no matter what! I knew that the Lord was in the plan. I managed to get through the first three years of college until 1950 when I was forced to return home to East Saint Louis to get a job because I desperately needed money. I found a job as a keypunch operator with the Army Finance Center in St. Louis.

I processed computer IBM cards from military pay records that computed military personnel credit and debit payments. The pay was good, and in 1951, before I could decide whether to return to Normal for my final year of college, the Air Force decided to open its own Accounting Center in Denver, CO. I was asked to transfer to this new center in Denver. I agreed to the move, never returning to school at ISNU.

Career

I came to Denver in 1951 with the Air Force Accounting and Finance Center. That date is rather historical in that the Air Force Accounting and Finance Center separated from the Army Finance Center, and I was among the first Air Force Accounting and Finance Center employees in

E.N.O.U.G.H.

Denver, Colorado. I was a GS1 keypunch operator. The Air Force Accounting and Finance Center opened its office on 38th and York Street in Denver.

I was also able to finish my education, getting my degree at Columbia College in Denver. I got my degree in Denver at Columbia College. My major was Business Administration. I thoroughly enjoyed Gregg's shorthand, which I use to this day. By the time I retired in 1994 after 42 years of service, I was an Accountant.

A Fantastic Hobby—And I Was Good At It! Golf

In the early 1950s, shortly after I started work at the Air Force Accounting Center, I developed an interest in golf. The men had a league, and I wanted to join. However, when I asked if I could join, they told me I should start a golfing club for women. And that is exactly what I did.

About a dozen of us played on Tuesdays after work at the Lowry Air Force Base Golf Course. We were having great fun! I discovered that there was a women's golf club started in the 1930s—the City Park Women's Golf Association (CPWGA). The group had been inactive for quite a while. So, in 1953, we revamped the organization. It was for women interested in golf, regardless of race, color or creed. When we were not playing at the Lowry Air Force Base Golf Course, we played at the Fitzsimmons Army Base Golf Course. Those were our only options for a while, as the city restricted where Black women and men could live and play.

As head of the CPWGA, I wanted to encourage young Black girls to play a sport from which they had been excluded and about which many were unfamiliar. The second goal was to encourage all women to play—those who had played before and were still interested and beginners who wanted to learn golf.

However, after we reactivated CPWGA, the City Park Golf Course contacted the group and encouraged our members to play golf at the City Park Golf Course. We jumped at the invitation. We never had trouble getting on the course. We would change into our golf clothes and cleats in the parking lot—of course, cleats are now banned. I always kept my clubs in my car in case I wanted to play.

I played golf until I could not. That time came only after I had a bout with the COVID-19 virus in March 2020, three months shy of my 90th birthday. I was hospitalized for 22 days. While it did not take away my desire to play, it sapped the energy I needed to play. By then, because I was nearly 90 years old, the virus slowed me down quite a bit.

Nonetheless, I have enjoyed golf for 60 years. I won awards over the years, so I guess I was a pretty good golfer. However, the trophies were not my main concern or purpose. I just loved to play golf and enjoy the outdoors. I have met a lot of wonderful people. I even got a chance to see Tiger Woods play twice. The first time, he was just a boy of ten or eleven, playing with his dad at City Park. His dad was stationed at Fitzsimmons Army base. I saw him again when he played in a tournament at City Park after he turned pro.

My Home

When I moved to Denver in the early 1950s, Blacks were not allowed to live beyond York Street in Denver or in hotels downtown, so I had to live with a Black family until I married. When I married in 1953, my husband and I moved into apartments in a segregated area of Denver.

We had a neighbor who was in Real Estate. In 1957, he sold us our home in Denver. By the time I sold my home early in 2024, I had lived there for 66 years. The preservation of the value of this house—from which I was threatened with eviction—and my experiences with those I believe were up to no good, ultimately trying to take my home, is why I write this book.

CHAPTER 3

Beware: Lessons Learned A Cautionary Tale for Senior Citizens

This book is about scams and cons, misrepresentations, and smooth-talking salespeople who take advantage of consumers—especially senior citizens—when we are alone, without the benefit of friends, family, and witnesses. Others have similar stories, and I want you to know you're not alone.[1] But many of us are either too traumatized by what has happened or ashamed—unnecessarily, I might add—to talk about what happened or admit that we have been victimized in this way. In addition, as in my case, the

---

1 Senior Scam Statistics 2024: Is Elder Fraud on the rise? (comparitech.com)

corporate conglomerates that should be helping to rectify or at least investigate the situation may not.[2]

So, I decided to tell you what happened to me. And my story is not easy to tell; it's complicated. But I assure you that I am not just an old lady with dementia and delusions. I am a woman of God, living my life. I have been blessed with children, friends, a home, and a desire to continue improving my life. Upon reflection on all of this, I realized that my biggest mistake was trusting people. I trusted in the goodness of others, and that trust was exploited.

Living My Life: This Was Nothing Unusual

As I said, just like all of you, I have been about the business of living my life, engaged in normal pursuits—nothing unusual. For instance, there is nothing unusual about buying a car at any age. Despite the rising prices, people do it every day. Keeping a nice home requires making periodic repairs and upgrades, and especially with long-term home ownership, there is nothing unusual about making those repairs and improvements using the equity in your home to do so. To that end, when low interest rates are of-

---

2 See https://finance.yahoo.com/news/maine-woman-65-loses-23k-110200406.html/#:~:text=Yahoo%20Finance,Back%20to%20classic (Detailing how a Maine woman was victimized by a scammer posing as a Bank of America employee; and the lack of assistance from Bank of America once the woman reported the scam).

fered, presuming they are legitimate, it only makes sense to take advantage of those offers. That is to be expected — that is why they are advertised.

Consumers should reasonably expect that representations made by loan companies regarding those low interest rates will be as represented in ads and the "large" print in contracts and not changed in the fine print of the same document. As you may know, Federal and state agencies (for example, the Federal Trade Commission and state Attorneys General offices) are established to protect consumers from fraud and misrepresentation by such companies, which includes hiding terms in the fine print with the intent to deceive us.

Finally, we know that many of us use our banks and credit unions to finance home renovations, car purchases, etc.[3]

The point is that the purchases I embarked upon in 2004 were no different and no more unusual than purchases made by hundreds of thousands of others. However, in my case, very little turned out as I expected or anticipated. Was I to blame? I don't think so. Was it because of my age? Perhaps, however, my journey is a warning for people of

---

3 I say this, but I also can't forget the history of banks and other financial institutions engaging in redlining — refusing home loans or charging exorbitant fees and interest rates to Black people — a practice that has plagued the Black community to this day.

all ages. Scams are rampant these days, affecting all of us, but perhaps most particularly the so-called "elderly."

So, again, this chapter is a cautionary tale for anybody who wants to keep living their lives, doing what everybody else wants to do to maintain that life, but whose age may be considered an opportunity to be taken advantage of.

Here's my story…

Retirement, Golf & Buying a Car

In 2004, at the age of 74, I was enjoying retirement. I had been retired for ten years, with a brief interlude as a paraprofessional with the Barrett Elementary School Reading Program in Denver. I also had a part-time position at my church, Shorter Community AME Church. At this point in my life, however, my focus was on enjoying golf. I had been playing golf since the 1950s, and as a member of the City Park Women's Golf Association (CPWGA) since 1953.

I had been living in my home for 47 years. In the 47 years since I purchased my home, I made repairs and renovations to the property, most of which I financed through the Public Service Credit Union (PSCU) using the equity in my home. So, in 2004, I was primarily considering buying a new car and a few additional home renovation projects. In anticipation of the car purchase, I saved half the down payment and intended to finance the balance. The monthly payments would be deducted from my pension. It was simple and straightforward . . . or so I thought.

One afternoon, while listening to KOA radio, the host - conservative radio and newspaper personality Mike Rosen - advertised a low interest fixed rate loan offered by American Financing Corporation (AFC), which he proclaimed he would recommend to his daughter. I became interested while listening to the commercial because I knew that the low interest rate (less than 2%) could work well with my car-buying plans and maybe even a home renovation I was planning. Of course, I had checked with other financial institutions, and nothing could compare with what Michael Rosen offered in the ad to the public. So, the offer was at least worth an inquiry.

I called the telephone number Rosen provided during the commercial. It was the number of the radio station. The person I spoke with told me he would give my contact information to AFC and that an AFC representative would call me. Very soon after my call to KOA radio, an AFC representative called and scheduled a visit to my home to discuss the loan.

An AFC representative arrived at my home on the scheduled day and time. I was alone in my home during the visit. The representative asked a lot of questions and took a great deal of personal and financial information. I know better now, but I had no qualms about providing all the requested information at the time. I had little debt—

E.N.O.U.G.H.

less than $200 from store credit cards—so I thought the questions were standard fare.

Let me say here that after what happened, I realized for both safety reasons and to have a witness to what occurred, I should have had a trusted friend, lawyer, or family member present when the AFC representative came to my home. I also would now not so freely provide the information requested without asking questions. In fact, it would have been best to have him leave the application with me so that I would have time to review it with someone I trust to fully understand its terms and what I was getting myself into.

A few days after his visit, the AFC representative called to tell me the loan was approved. After canceling a scheduled appointment at my home to answer any lingering questions I had before I signed the closing documents, he appeared at my part-time job at Shorter, presenting me with only the signature page of the closing documents to sign. Importantly, that page did not state the loan amount.

I was too trusting. I should have insisted that we meet when I was not otherwise occupied and had a friend, relative, or legal representative present during any meeting—whether in my home or elsewhere. And, of course, I should have insisted that the AFC representative provide me with the full closing documents—including the total loan amount—before I signed anything. As I was busy with my duties at the Church, I hurriedly signed a document—the signature page—that did not include all the relevant information, trusting that all previous representations were true. They were not. I learned never to be in a hurry to sign any document with financial consequences. Such haste will most assuredly lead to mistakes.

The mistake became very apparent when I discovered the loan amount was more than $140,000.00. It included the remaining amount I owed to Rickenbaugh Cadillac for the car I purchased. That was certainly what I intended. But that balance was less than $20,000. What I did not expect, request, or intend is that this loan would include other outstanding debt—particularly since it was debt I disputed and amounted to 80% of the loan. The outstanding debt was allegedly owed to PSCU. Interestingly, although these amounts were allegedly outstanding, PSCU could not provide any documentation to prove the debt. I requested the loan documents from PSCU, which would substantiate its claim that I had taken out those loans and had a balance of $88,000.00. The PSCU representative advised me those documents were no longer available. In his words, that history had "fallen off." Specifically, he told me that loan records were only kept for five (5) years. I found that interesting and convenient for PSCU as it could allege loans were taken out, but if challenged more than five years later—even though allegedly not paid off—they did not have to prove it.

E.N.O.U.G.H.

About My Car

The car I purchased—a Cadillac Deville—cost approximately $34,000. I had a down payment of $20,000, leaving a balance, as reflected on the AFC application, of approximately $17k after taxes, fees, and warranty charges. However, somehow, the $17,000 balance became $55,000. When pressed, PSCU representatives (as you will see, PSCU was the last entity holding the loan) advised me that $55,000 would be paid to GMAC for a warranty that accompanied my car purchase. While I purchased an extended warranty when I purchased the car, note that today, in 2024, the maximum cost for a Cadillac extended warranty is $4700. So, while I am certain how much the car cost, how much of a down payment I made, and that I made payments from my pension to GMAC, I have no idea how much Rickenbach/GMAC was ultimately paid, when, or by whom. PSCU has been unable or unwilling to provide any documentation to answer those questions. Rickenbach was no help in that regard.[4] Yet, as I stated, in 2024, PSCU, which had changed its name to Canvas, claimed I still owed $171,000 on the loan. And none of the entities I did business with have any records.

---

4 Several years after the purchase, when I was attempting to piece all of this together, when I confronted the then-current Rickenbaugh sales manager about the whole matter, he responded that he was nine years old when all of this happened.

Explaining "Everything"

It is crucial to understand that I never personally received any money that was the subject of the AFC loan. I was told it was all used to pay existing debt, a result that was certainly not my intention when I was considering the AFC loan. I realized this early on and immediately questioned an AFC representative about the loan. Their solution was to send someone to my home to "explain everything." This experience left me feeling misled about the true nature of the loan, emphasizing the need for honesty and integrity in financial transactions.

Two people from the title company came to my home, one of whom was an African American woman. Perhaps they thought her presence would provide some comfort, but she did not actively participate in the conversation. Unfortunately, once again, I was alone when they arrived, and I felt no more reassured when they left. Whether intentionally or unintentionally, they left with my copy of the loan application, which they were using to "explain everything." Despite my protests, neither the title company representatives nor anyone else ever provided me with another copy of the application. This experience left me completely in the dark, underscoring the need for support and guidance in complex financial matters.

E.N.O.U.G.H.

Selling My Loan: A Common Practice

There is no guarantee that the financial institution—bank, credit union, or finance company—with which you enter a loan will retain and manage the loan throughout the life of the loan until it is fully paid. I LEARNED that it is, in fact, quite common for one financial institution to sell your loan to another over the life of the loan. In most cases, as the mortgagee, you have no control over whether this occurs. In my case, I was saddled with a loan I was disputing when AFC almost immediately sold the loan. In fact, over the first eight months of the loan, it was repeatedly sold to other financial entities—with a higher interest rate each time the loan was sold. That selling the loan was permissible was buried in the fine print. There were several other things I LEARNED.

Regarding the interest rate, I LEARNED that the first page of the application showed an interest rate of 1.75%--which was consistent with my expectation. However, I LEARNED that another rate of 5.245% was listed elsewhere in the contract. Further, a box for "VARIABLE RATE" is checked in smaller type. This loan was apparently always an adjustable-rate mortgage loan (ARM), which could be changed monthly with a maximum interest rate of 19.900%, a far cry from the 1.75% I thought I was receiving for the life of the loan. Finally, the contract permitted payments to increase after the first five years to almost double the original payment amount. These "hidden" terms explained – but did not justify—why the rate on the loan continued to rise. This reality was quite different than what Mike Rosen communicated in the advertisement on KOA radio. Did he know? Would he really recommend this to his daughter if he did?

Reverse Mortgages: Should You Really Trust Tom Selleck?

In those first eight months, I paid the loan down from $148,000.00 to $137,000.00—paying approximately $1375 monthly. As rates rose, I became concerned that I could not make the payments and would lose my home. A mortgage modification in the form of a reverse mortgage loan was suggested to me as a way to avoid such an outcome.

I followed instructions for financial counseling with the Northeast Denver Housing Center (NDHC). Such counseling was required before qualifying for a reverse mortgage. I was disappointed by the lack of information I received from NDHC, which directed me to Universal Lending to process the reverse mortgage. Rather than saving money, I had to borrow 20K to pay for fees and other costs for a reverse mortgage. That experience was, in my opinion, another scam and/or certainly not full disclosure. Universal Lending charged me $15,166.25 in fees to obtain the reverse mortgage. In the interim, NDHC placed a $19,000.00 lien against my home, which was only removed when I questioned an NDHC supervisor about the lien.

E.N.O.U.G.H.

Reverse Mortgages

Tom Selleck and the problems with the housing market in the early part of the 21st century gave consumers the idea that reverse mortgages were worthwhile options to avoid foreclosure and allow them/us to stay in our homes. However, many—including myself—ultimately discovered that reverse mortgages were not the advertised panacea.

I determined that in utilizing the reverse mortgage, ownership of my home was no longer necessarily in my control. I wanted to leave the home for my children. With a reverse mortgage, I realized that would only happen if, upon my demise, the loan was completely paid off. Thus, I went to Colorado Legal Services when I understood that I would continue to have problems with Universal Lending and the reverse mortgage—another roadblock. I was advised that because one of the Legal Services board members was an employee of Universal Lending Colorado, Legal Services could not help me. At least, that is what I was told.

With that bit of unhelpful news, I believed my only option was switching from a reverse mortgage to a conventional loan. I refinanced the reverse mortgage (that had by this time been sold to HUD) to a conventional loan with PSCU (now Canvas Credit Union). Yes, PSCU, the source of many of my problems. But what is the saying, "It's better to deal with the devil you know than the devil you don't."

That was my thought process. Having engaged with several financial institutions already, and with a better understanding of corporate greed, I went back to PSCU. Ultimately, it was a decision I regretted, but it was the only one I thought I could make at the time.

The rate for this new conventional loan was 3.75%; however, it was still an ARM. Interestingly, despite regular payments for over a decade, I was advised that in order to opt for a conventional loan in 2016, the amount of the loan would now be $200,000.00!

Who Will Listen?

As I said earlier, I have not waited until now to complain about this ill-fated financial journey. At the end of the book, I provide a list of resources available to consumers who have or believe they have been victimized by scams, cons, and the like. I do not provide those recommendations without prior experience.

I have contacted my political representatives and every agency—local, state, and federal—for help over the last twenty years without success. I have hired several attorneys to help me through this trauma without result. Of late, my efforts in making these contacts have been characterized in a negative light, apparently to undermine my credibility. Undoubtedly, all but a few assume that I am just an old woman with dementia, easily victimized by scams and unable to manage my finances. Scores of seniors and non-seniors have been scammed for thousands of dollars. That is the world in which we live. However, it seems that only when we are senior citizens is there a "blame the victim" mentality, resulting in a tendency to dismiss the validity and integrity of our claims. This effort to undermine my credibility seemed to be working—at least for a while.

A Conservatorship

I believe that I was placed in a conservatorship because I ultimately refused to make loan payments. For several months prior, I wrote "in protest" on the monthly payment checks. Eventually, I had enough and just stopped paying. They contacted my daughter, Cheri, to see if she could convince me to pay. When she could not, she paid the note for a few months—not wanting me to lose my home, which is the threat PSCU hung over our heads.

In March, my money and I were placed in a conservatorship. The Court approved the conservatorship even though the Court Visitor who interviewed me stated that,

> "The respondent's home was clean and organized. She appeared appropriately groomed. She stated various people bring her meals, clean, and care for her lawn. At interview the respondent was friendly and oriented to self, place, and time."

So, I was in my right mind at the time of the interview. However, perhaps because the Court Visitor was already aware of the allegations made in favor of the conservatorship, in the same document, he then went on to say,

> "Her representations about the situation with her finances and health were confusing and tainted with conspiracy-laden stories of fake and stolen documents, lawsuits and cover ups."

Nonetheless, as to my ability to "manage my financial functions," he states:

> "It is unclear if she is having difficulty managing her finances beyond her home."

So, he was not sure if I could manage my money and admitted in his preamble that the basis of this whole conservatorship seems to be that I began to make payments of the loan in protest over the last year. Yes, as I said, beginning in January of 2023, I stopped paying on what I believed to be a fraudulent loan. Had my objections to the loan been recent, perhaps the suggestion of some diminished capacity would seem reasonable. However, I am a former accountant and have been challenging the integrity of this loan for 20 years! Thus, how these facts subjected me to a permanent conservatorship, where a law firm has total control over my money, is beyond me. As an aside, based on the fees of the law firm acting as my conservator, I feared I would quickly have little money left for my care.

It is worth noting that the conservatorship was approved without any medical verification that I could not handle my affairs. While the Court initially ordered that the hearing would not go forward without a letter from my doctor regarding my mental state, the Court rescinded the order after those seeking to establish the conservatorship filed a motion for it to do so. For his part, the Court Visitor[5] who interviewed me stated that my doctor did not return his calls. While the petition to rescind the order for a doctor's letter suggests the Court Visitor made numerous calls that were not returned, there is no supporting evidence that he did so. The Court Visitor did not state how many calls he made, dates, times, and whether he left a message about the nature of his calls. Despite this lack of information, which appears to be the only real basis for the motion, the Court rescinded its earlier order requiring a doctor's letter. Also, it seems there is a law in Colorado

---

5 The court will assign a person known as a Court Visitor to investigate the necessity of the conservatorship and whether the person asking to be the guardian is an appropriate choice. The Court Visitor will review paperwork filed with the court and conduct interviews as necessary.

that does not require medical substantiation for a person to be placed in conservatorship. That law makes it easier to rush somebody like me—at this point, I was 92—into a conservatorship.

The Court Visitor recommended the conservatorship, stating that less restrictive means were unavailable and that there should be no restrictions on the conservator's powers and duties over my assets. First, I am unaware that less restrictive means –financial advisor, accountant, etc.— were ever suggested or explored by anyone. It is as if those involved (including the police who sent a letter saying I am a nuisance) are acting on behalf of PSCU/Canvas—because my questions about the 19-year-old loan appear to be the only focus of the conservatorship. No objection or outrage was expressed because it appears I paid for my car twice. There is no evidence I have not paid all my other bills and managed all other financial matters. It all evolves around the loan. That is curious to me. And while I continue to hold tight to my faith, this all seems very unfair.

When I objected to the conservatorship, the Court appointed an attorney to represent me in my challenge. However, after this new attorney consulted with the firm seeking a permanent conservatorship, "my" attorney withdrew from my case. I am not sure her area of expertise is advocating for someone challenging a conservatorship. She may have also thought so, as she told the Court I needed a guardian ad litem appointed. She said she talked to me several times. She did not say I was uncooperative or could not communicate with her. She never explained in the motion—or to me—why she could not proceed as my attorney or why a guardian ad litem was preferable, except to say she "is not able to develop an attorney-client relationship with Respondent." She was not required to explain that statement, and it is hard to believe that anybody—including the Court—could articulate what she meant. It was just a standard motion filed when an attorney wants to be removed from a matter. The motion she filed was unopposed; however, she admits in her motion that I opposed the appointment of a guardian ad litem. We did agree on one thing. She told the Court I needed an attorney to represent me; she just did not want to be that person. The Court did not appoint another attorney to act on my behalf.

I wonder why everyone was in such a hurry to place my money in conservatorship.

Update:

The good news is that the court-appointed Conservator is out of the picture, and my daughter has assumed the role of my guardian. At least control of my money is in the family!

Because my physical condition was declining, and I was living alone, even while under the thumb of the Court-appointed conservator, I wanted to sell my home and use the money to move into a senior living facility. The facility I was most interested in would allow me to have my own apartment with most of the amenities I experienced in my home. In addition, they provide my meals, which are served in a dining room for all residents. I knew that would allow me to meet new people and engage in new activities. In addition, there is also an assisted living facility to which I can transfer if and when I need it.

I had money in savings and decided to go forward with the move before selling my house. It was a wonderful decision. My needs are being met while I am still relatively independent. The food is good, and I am learning to play bridge!

Selling My House

I knew I could not bear the expense of these new living accommodations without selling my house. However, I was concerned about selling my house while I was under the control of the conservator, fearing that the fees and other expenses, in addition to the Conservator fees, would consume a good portion of the equity I could receive from the sale. With God's blessings, those fears were allayed when my daughter replaced the court-appointed conservator and took on the responsibilities as my guardian.

But . . .

So, there is good news, but the not-so-good news is that my issues were not resolved in the end. I guess my daughter thought it would reduce my stress and that I could put it all behind me. Whatever her reasoning, she strongly urged me to settle my dispute with PSCU by paying off the loan amount it claimed I still owed – a whopping $171,000.00!

So, after 20 years of disputing what I thought would be a small fixed-rate loan, and after paying thousands of dollars on the loan, I still owed more than the original loan. I know "financing" means you pay more than the original loan amount, but tens of thousands of dollars more?! If you ask my opinion, it is unfair, usurious, and unconscionable!

What Did I Want, and What Did I Get

The only reason I called KOA about the advertised loan was to use the equity in my home to finance the purchase of a $34000 car. It is, after all, an accepted method of buying a car. I went to AFC rather than my bank or credit Union because they advertised a less than 2% fixed-rate loan. That was the best rate offered at the time. Once approved for the approximately $20000.00 loan, I intended to make monthly payments on the 2% loan from my pension. Several things have become apparent over my 20-year odyssey.

1. It appears that the loan amount I wanted to finance was not enough—for AFC. I only asked for financing of approximately $20k, the balance owed on the car. I

never sought financing for any other outstanding debt, as I had none. I intended to use any additional loan amount for which I qualified for additional repairs on my home. However, as I've stated, I never saw a dime of that money! The entire loan amount was used to pay others for debt, which I insist I never incurred. More importantly, it was never my intent to do anything other than finance the purchase of my car at a low, fixed interest rate.

2. The loan was not a 1.175% fixed-rate loan that AFC was offering. I only discovered after I signed the closing documents that per the fine print, to which I was never directed, it was instead an Adjustable Rate Mortgage (ARM) that could go up as high as 19.99% according to the paperwork (although at the time, in Colorado the maximum amount was 18%—still a far cry from the 1.175% that was being advertised and on which I relied).

3. Scams, cons, and misrepresentations don't only emanate from "shady" individuals in too-large suits who are sweating a lot and chain-smoking cigarettes. Banks, credit unions, and other financial institutions and finance companies—corporate conglomerates—play a huge role--whether it's redlining, important or contradictory terms hidden in the fine print, or advertisements and commercials that only provide you with

E.N.O.U.G.H.

some of the information, none or only a small portion of which is relevant. Sometimes it's not what they say, and sometimes it is what they don't.

4. Despite Tom Selleck's sincere assurances that he would not recommend a reverse mortgage unless he believed in it, I don't believe in them. They can cost considerable out-of-pocket money, and you could lose your home.

In fact, any option can be expensive. I could not keep the AFC loan because the interest rates could have reached 19.99%. When I feared losing my home because I could not pay the skyrocketing payments and took out the reverse mortgage, the loan amount was $137,000. My choice of a reverse mortgage cost me more than $20,000, which I could only afford by taking out another loan. When I once again feared losing my home and being unable to leave it to my children, I refinanced to a conventional loan with a lower interest rate (still an ARM, though). To my shock and surprise, the amount owed was now, 13 years later, $200000.00. When I finally acquiesced and paid the loan off after selling my house in 2024, the payoff was a whopping $171,000.00.

Whatever the impact, I ended all of this positively: First, I got out of the conservatorship. I would much rather have my daughter supervising my financial affairs than people I don't know charging fees I did not want to afford.

    Secondly, and more importantly, I have been able to repair my relationship with my daughter, whom I dearly love. I know that the credit union bringing her into the fray when I stopped paying the mortgage caused a strain on our relationship. I know she only acted in what she believed was my best interest when she pressured me to settle with PSCU/Canvas and pay them what they claimed I owed. It would, she believed, reduce my stress and remove this huge burden I had been carrying for twenty years. In that regard, I suppose she is right. I am relieved to have closure. That said, I will always believe I was victimized by all the financial institutions and corporations involved. Nonetheless, having my daughter by my side as I approach the middle of my 90th decade is a blessing for which I am eternally grateful.

CHAPTER 4

Takeaways For Seniors and All Victims

In the end, despite believing that I was taken advantage of—scammed—on several fronts, I discovered few avenues of redress. I do not think my experience is a solitary one. Unfortunately, I imagine many others have been similarly victimized.

I can share two perspectives on all that has happened. One is an analogy to a fundamental problem we are confronted with today; the other is more personal.

For some, the analogy may seem extreme. However, as I reflect on my journey of discord, I am reminded of George Floyd. And I think stealing what a poor man has is the same as putting your knee on their neck and squeezing the last drop of humanity from the person who has worked hard for the little they have been allowed to gain.

E.N.O.U.G.H.

The more personal reflection is from a conversation with my doctor in 2019. I was 89 years old and continually stressed out by everything I described. My primary care physician at the time asked me if I felt suicidal. I told him no, but I would like to kill the people who put me in this scandalous scam. As a result, I was on anxiety medication, and I had been diagnosed with the beginning stages of dementia—all because I heard a two-minute commercial on a radio station that I now know was too good to be true. You can only push someone so far before they break.

That being the case, the only thing left for me to do is to tell you, my readers—particularly seniors—what I have learned and make suggestions for how they may avoid the pitfalls I have experienced.

My Questions

This dreadful situation leaves me with the following questions:

1. Why have I been put through "The Gates of Hell" mentally and physically starting in 2004 because of a scam related to my loan application?

2. Why did my copies of the loan application and approval disappear from my home after visits from title company representatives?

Takeaways For Seniors and All Victims

3. Why is it legal to sell an Adjusted Rate Mortgage month after month? My loan was sold at least four times. Each time it was sold, the interest rate increased. Nonetheless, I paid over $11,000.00 on the loan during those first eight months.

4. Why did American Financing Corporation pay $88,000.00 to Public Service Federal Credit Union and $ 55,000.00 to GMAC's Rickenbaugh Cadillac through now-defunct First Magnus Financial, Arizona?

5. Why are there allegations that PSCU loaned me $91,800.00 and then loaned me $97,300.00, but no documents to support those allegations or the demand for payment that followed? PSCU states that corresponding deposits from loans posted against my account are outside of the statute of limitations, but the loans are still there.

6. Why did the financial entity responsible for the reverse mortgage charge me $15,166.25 for a Reverse Mortgage, disputing my equity of 48 years, knowing I had to borrow the money to pay this charge and thereafter quickly selling the reverse mortgage for $137,000.00 to another Loan Company?

7. Why did Rickenbaugh Cadillac deny receiving a down payment of $22,000.00, other payments of $55,000.00,

E.N.O.U.G.H.

and monthly deductions of $322.00 for a 2004 Deville Cadillac?

8. What evidence exists to put me/my money in conservatorship?

9. Why can't I protest what I believe to be an invalid loan?

I have received very few answers to the questions I raise. However, I have some advice for seniors—and anyone for that matter—doing business with any financial institutions and engaged in any transactions:

My Advice:

1. You need a witness: Always have someone with you when discussing any business matter.

2. Never sign anything without showing it to an attorney or adult relative you trust first.

3. Do not invite/allow people into your home who want to sell you anything!

4. Have an accountant to manage your books when possible. These are records you may need later—especially if records held by financial institutions no longer exist.

5. From lotteries to reverse mortgages: Be wary of anything that sounds too good to be true, even if hawked by celebrities, it may be.

6. Never sign any document without seeing the whole document and understanding it thoroughly. It is okay and very important to ask questions until you do understand.

7. If you are scammed, report the scam. One report indicated that fewer than 15% of scam victims report the scam to their local police or relevant local, state, or national consumer protection agencies.

8. Speak up/share your experiences with other seniors.

9. Realize that the older we get, the less people believe us and the more they think we suffer from Alzheimer's or some form of dementia. We must continually prove we are lucid and sane--particularly when accusing younger people of wrongdoing. Of course, we can be forgetful, but does that make us crazy?

What to do If This Happens to You: Resources

I have not waited until now to complain about the injustices, misrepresentations, and general dishonesty I encountered on this journey. I fought with the finance companies, banks, and the justice system and contacted legislators and local, state, and federal agencies. Nonetheless, just because I received no satisfaction for my 20-year journey through the fire and brimstone of corporations, financial institutions, and the courts does not mean your experience will be the same. The best-case scenario, of course, is to avoid these scams and cons and fine print altogether. I hope the advice I provided above will make avoidance the more likely outcome. However, if you find yourself waist-deep in a scam, con, fraud, or engaged with uncooperative financial institutions, I have listed some resources to which you can go for assistance:

1. **Legal Services/Legal Aid:** Most legal services offices have an Elder law component that is free and not dependent on your income. So, if you have a question about a legal transaction, consult your local Legal Aid/Legal Services Office.

2. **Federal Trade Commission** (ReportFraud.ftc.gov). Locally, go to ftc.gov/exploredata.gov.

3. **State Attorneys General Offices:** Most have a consumer protection or consumer fraud unit.

4. **County District Attorney Offices:** If you think you have been a victim of a crime, in addition to filing a police report (#10 below), contact your county district

Takeaways For Seniors and All Victims

attorney's office. Each usually has a Victim's Witness, a Victim's Assistance, or a Consumer Protection Division.

5. **Local, state, and federal representatives** (from City Council to State representatives and senators to the U.S. Congress). Know who they are and demand accountability!

6. **AARP Fraud Watch Network Hotline** (877-908-3360): Volunteers are available to advise you if you are unsure of the best next steps in a fraud situation.

7. **Stolen Identity:** (identitytheft.gov) Contact this site for a list of steps to take.

8. **Financial Crimes** (finra.org) website of the Financial Regulatory Authority (not a government agency). This site provides a "Recovery Checklist for Victims of Investment Fraud."

9. Report compromised/stolen credit cards and debit cards to the issuing financial institution as soon as possible, asking them to reverse the transaction and refund the money taken. **Note:** It is best not to give your debit card to anyone or allow it to be used. It is instant money, and the odds of recovery drop dramatically. If you use a credit card instead, you can challenge a charge.

E.N.O.U.G.H.

10. **Police Report.** Always file a police report if your property has been stolen or you believe you are the victim of fraud or a scam. Doing so is essential to make an insurance claim on stolen property.

11. **Consumer Protection Agencies:** Go to usa.gov for a list of consumer protection agencies and other relevant agencies not listed above.

12. **The American Institute of Certified Public Accountants** (AICPA) assists Elder Financial Planning. Go to: *https://us.aicpa.org/content/dam/aicpa/interestareas/personalfinancialplanning/resources/elderplanningservices/downloadabledocuments/health-care-coverage-planning-5th-excerpt.pdf;* or *https://us.aicpa.org/interestareas/personalfinancialplanning/resources/elderplanningservices*

CHAPTER 5

———

Enjoying Life In My 90s Leaving Stress Behind

As this book goes to press, I am 94 years old. I am learning how to play bridge and enjoying the new friends I have made in my new senior housing. As the days pass and taking care of myself becomes more of a challenge—it takes forever just for me to dress myself! —I admit I am beginning to consider transferring to the assisted living facility on site. There is no need for sadness or pity; this is all a part of life. And despite the trials and tribulations I have shared with you over these pages, my life has been good. I am blessed in so many ways, but most particularly by putting my faith in God. He has carried me through.

I hope none of you will endure a journey like mine, but

E.N.O.U.G.H.

I know some of you will. Have courage and have faith and all will be well.

God Bless!

Alruth Toney

www.ingramcontent.com/pod-product-compliance
Lightning Source LLC
Chambersburg PA
CBHW061731070526
44583CB00024B/3101